My First

First Visit to the Dentist

Monica Hughes

Raintree

Chicago, Illinois

© 2004 Raintree
Published by Raintree, a division of Reed Elsevier, Inc.
Chicago, Illinois
Customer Service 888-363-4266
Visit our website at www.raintreelibrary.com

Printed and bound in the United States at Lake Book Manufacturing, Inc.
07 06 05 04 03
10 9 8 7 6 5 4 3 2 1

Library of Congress Cataloging-in-Publication Data:
Hughes, Monica.
  First visit to the dentist / Monica Hughes.
    p. cm. -- (My first)
Includes bibliographical references and index.
Contents: Going to the dentist -- In the waiting room -- Meeting the
dentist -- The dentist gets ready -- The check-up -- Clean and polish --
Brushing teeth -- Problem teeth -- Well done! -- The next appointment.
  ISBN 1-4109-0645-0 (Library Binding-hardcover) -- ISBN 1-4109-0671-X (Pbk)
  1. Dentistry--Juvenile literature. 2. Children--Preparation for
dental care--Juvenile literature. [1. Dental care. 2. Destistry.] I.
Title. II. Series: Hughes, Monica. My first.
  RK63.H846 2004
  617.6--dc21
                              2003011054

Acknowledgments
The Publishers would like to thank the following for permission to reproduce photographs: pp. 4, 5, 6, 8, 9, 10, 11, 12,
13, 14, 15, 16, 17, 18, 20, 21, 22, 23 Gareth Boden; p. 7 Rob Judges; p. 19 Science Photo Library/Alex Bartel

Cover photograph is reproduced with permission of Gareth Boden

Every effort has been made to contact copyright holders of any material reproduced in this book.
Any omissions will be rectified in subsequent printings if notice is given to the publishers.

Some words are shown in bold, **like this.** You can find out
what they mean by looking in the glossary on page 24.

Contents

Going to the Dentist

Today I am going to the dentist. So, I brush my teeth.

Here we are at the dentist's office.

His name is Dr. Singh.

In the Waiting Room

We meet the **receptionist.**

We can read or play
in the waiting room.

Meeting the Dentist

I meet Dr. Singh.
I sit in his big chair.

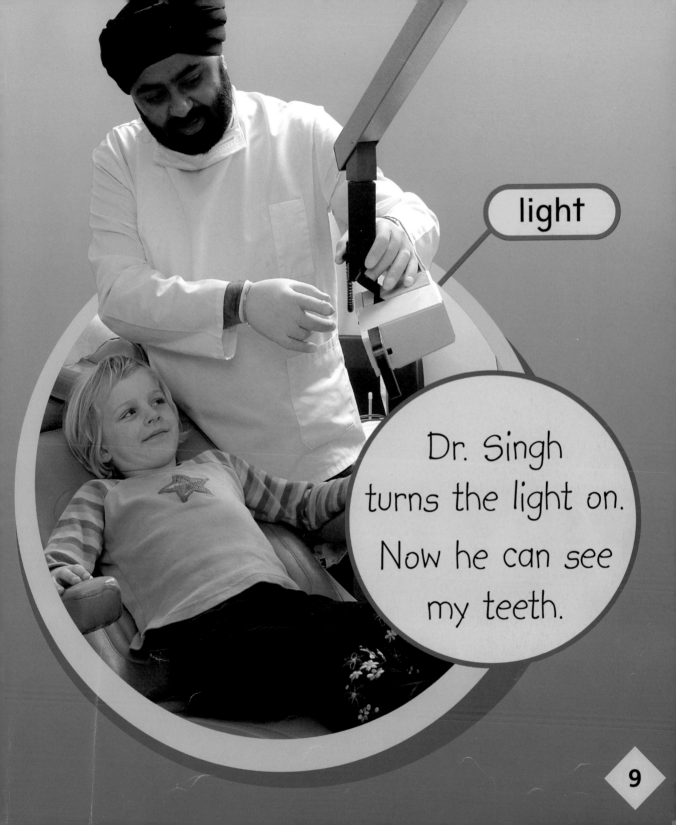

light

Dr. Singh
turns the light on.
Now he can see
my teeth.

9

Getting Ready

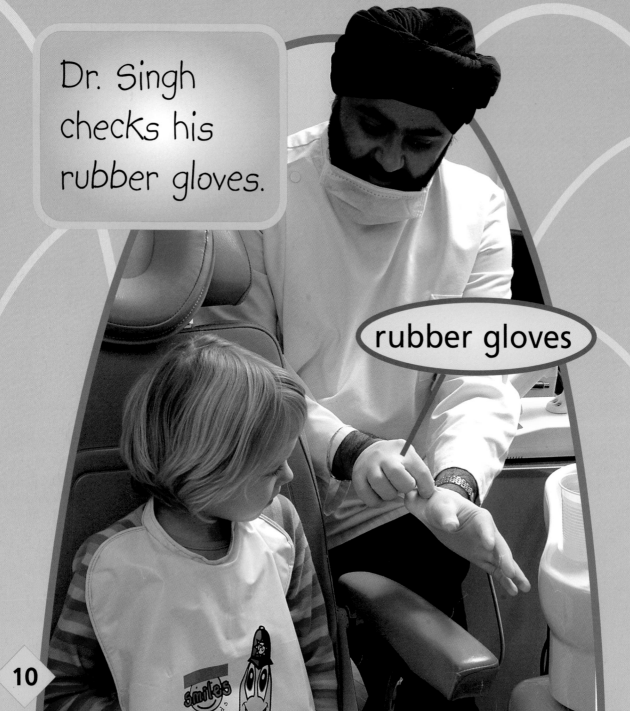

Dr. Singh checks his rubber gloves.

rubber gloves

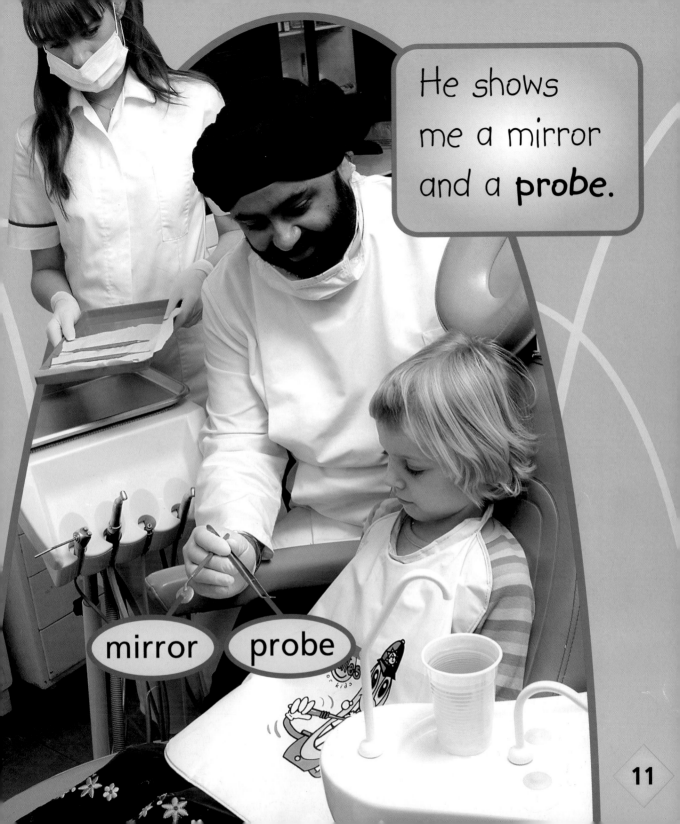

The Checkup

safety glasses

I wear **safety glasses.**

Dr. Singh looks at my teeth with the mirror.

He finds a **cavity** with the **probe**.
The **assistant** writes it in my **chart**.

Fixing Teeth

Dr. Singh fixes the **cavity**.

He says I may need braces.

Clean and Shiny

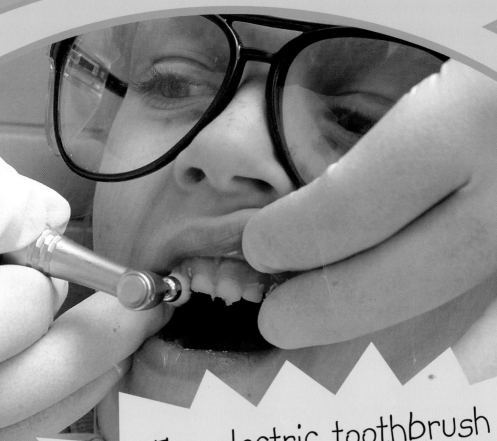

Dr. Singh cleans my teeth.

The electric toothbrush buzzes and tickles.

The **assistant** helps me rinse my mouth.
Now my teeth are clean and shiny.

17

Brushing My Teeth

Dr. Singh shows me how to brush my teeth.

Now I can brush my teeth the right way.

19

All Done!

The **assistant** helps me choose a sticker.

The **receptionist** gives
me a new toothbrush.

Time to Go

We make an appointment.

I will eat good food to keep my teeth healthy.

23

Glossary

assistant   a person who helps in an office

braces   metal and plastic parts that a dentist puts on your teeth to make them straighter

cavity   a hole in a tooth

chart   papers that a dentist or doctor keeps that show how you are each time you visit

probe   metal tool that a dentist uses to check your teeth for cavities

receptionist   person who works in an office answering phones, meeting people, and making appointments

safety glasses   glasses that protect your eyes

Index